photos
STYLE RECIPES

photos
STYLE RECIPES

photography DAVID MATHESON

styling MICHAEL WALTERS

text SAMANTHA MOSS

style consultant JASON STEWART

executive editor CLAY IDE

A Fireside Book
Published by Simon & Schuster
New York   London   Toronto   Sydney

the creative possibilities of photos

A baby's first steps. A vivid Parisian postcard. Your parents' wedding day. Displayed in creative ways, photographs tell the rich story of who we are, and turn the people and events we cherish into a living part of every day. This book is just a glimpse at some of the ways in which photos can bring passion, beauty, and humor to every room in your home.

At Pottery Barn, we believe that ease and inspiration are the soul of style. We designed our *Style Recipes* books with the belief that your home can be a unique expression of who you are, changing and evolving along with you over time. We shoot all of our photography in real homes, often in one day, so our ideas must always be accessible and simple to accomplish. Every photo-display recipe in these pages is fun to make and easy to achieve. We hope that our creations will inspire you to come up with your own personal twists — or entirely new ideas altogether.

WELDON OWEN

Chief Executive Officer John Owen
President & Chief Operating Officer Terry Newell
Vice President, Publisher Roger Shaw
Vice President, International Sales Stuart Laurence

Creative Director Gaye Allen
Business Manager Richard Van Oosterhout
Associate Publisher Shawna Mullen
Senior Art Director Emma Boys
Managing Editor Sarah Lynch
Production Director Chris Hemesath
Production Manager Todd Rechner
Color Manager Teri Bell
Photo Coordinator Elizabeth Lazich

Photos Style Recipes was conceived and produced by
Weldon Owen Inc.
814 Montgomery Street, San Francisco, CA 94133
in collaboration with Pottery Barn
3250 Van Ness Avenue, San Francisco, CA 94109

Set in Praxis EF™ and Formata™

Color separations by International Color Services
Printed in Singapore by Tien Wah Press (Pte.) Ltd.

A WELDON OWEN PRODUCTION

Fireside
A Division of Simon & Schuster, Inc.
1230 Avenue of the Americas
New York, NY 10020

10 9 8 7 6 5 4 3 2 1

Library of Congress Cataloging-in-Publication data is available

ISBN-13: 978-1-4165-7100-1
ISBN-10:   1-4165-7100-0

contents

FRAMING AND MATTING TECHNIQUES TO SHOWCASE YOUR IMAGES; AND

COMPOSITION WHEN YOU ARE selecting photos

ORGANIZE YOUR PHOTO COLLECTION WITH A TRIED-AND-TRUE FORMULA: CATEGORIZE, CONSOLIDATE, CONTAIN

Chances are, there are lost works of art hiding deep in your closets, cabinets, and drawers. Boxes filled with snapshots or envelopes bulging with prints can easily become like buried treasure, packed away and long forgotten. Restore order and bring special memories out of hiding by applying this simple rule: categorize, consolidate, contain.

Start by separating your photos into categories by date, person, or event. Then consolidate them in one place, such as on a shelf or in a filing system. Next, contain your images so they're protected and easy to locate. There's an endless selection of products available – the trick is to choose a system you'll use. Tins and paper bands, like those pictured here, are handy for bundling groups of travel photos. Albums, scrapbooks, interleaving folders for prints and negatives, and archival photo boxes are also excellent photo storage options.

SMART STORAGE SYSTEMS PROTECT IMAGES, INVITE BROWSING, AND KEEP PHOTOS AT YOUR FINGERTIPS

Photo storage should offer long-term protection against exposure that can damage images. Light fades photographs over time, and humidity breaks down their paper backing. Acid and the plant fiber lignin, two substances found in most papers, are the other great enemies of photos. To prolong the life of your photos, choose archival-quality or acid-neutral photo storage boxes, albums, and scrapbooks.

Archival-quality tape, pens, markers, and photo corners are essential for mounting photos in albums and scrapbooks. Placing photos on acid-neutral backing is not enough, as photos will become brittle and break where they are attached to the pages unless you use archival tape or photo corners to affix them.

Souvenirs make wonderful additions to albums. As you mount ticket stubs, postcards, and other keepsake items in an album, be sure to place them so that they will not touch your photos directly. This will help to keep your images safe and well preserved long into the future.

Archival photo albums (opposite); acid-neutral scrapbook (top); archival-quality photo-mounting supplies organized in a modular tray (bottom)

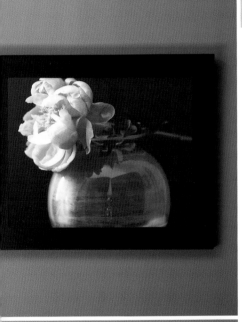

USE CROPPING, BORDERS, AND MATS TO TELL A STORY AND TO HIGHLIGHT KEY ELEMENTS IN A PHOTO

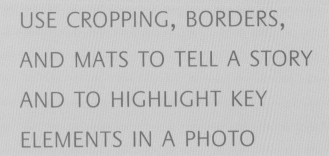

Cropping lets you try out creative ways to call attention to your images. Some photos have background objects or other details that can compete with the subject. Cropping helps you highlight the essential elements of the photo and eliminate anything that doesn't belong. To look at different crops, use four lengths of black construction paper and place them over the image, like a window, to hide or reveal various details. Look for sharply focused images with plenty of visual information, such as groups of people or multiple objects.

Mats emphasize certain details of a photo, too. Traditional mats center the image and allow it to float slightly toward the top of frame. This creates a formal effect. Other options include using a large mat to emphasize a small picture, "bleeding" a picture to the frame edge for a modern, graphic look, and floating a picture between panes of glass in a frame.

Classic, formal photo mat (opposite); emphasizing a small image with a large mat (top); bleeding an image to the frame (middle); floating an image (bottom)

FOUND OBJECTS AND JUST ABOUT ANYTHING WITH COMPARTMENTS, LIKE THIS HOTEL KEY CUPBOARD, CAN BECOME INTRIGUING PHOTO FRAMES

photo gallery wall

HERE'S A SIMPLE TECHNIQUE FOR HANGING A WALL OF PICTURES
WITHOUT LEAVING A COLLECTION OF MISPLACED NAIL HOLES IN YOUR
WAKE. PAPER TEMPLATES LET YOU TRY OUT DIFFERENT ARRANGEMENTS.

picture hangers

• Nails lose some of their holding power the day after you install them, once the effects of gravity take over. For heavy pictures, opt for wall-cleat systems or three-nail picture hooks.

• Sawtooth picture hangers won't support much weight but are ideal for enabling small frames to lay flat against the wall.

working with templates

4 black, medium-edge frames, 9 x 9 in (23 x 23 cm), 9 x 12 in (23 x 30 cm), 12 x 12 in (30 x 30 cm), 12 x 18 in (30 x 45 cm) • gray mats • 1 roll of brown kraft paper • scissors • blue painter's tape • measuring tape • carpenter's level

Try this photo-hanging technique that gallery pros use. First, trace the frames on kraft paper and cut out the shapes. On the back of each frame, pull the picture-hanging wire up until it's taut and measure from the peak of the wire to the top of the frame. On the corresponding kraft paper shape, measure the same distance from the top edge and mark the spot with an X. Lay the picture hook on the paper so that the bottom of the hook touches the center of the X, then mark the paper where the nail hole for the hook will go.

one Make black-and-white
copies of each image in a few
different sizes and then try out
several crops inside the mats.
Select the ones you like best.

two Trace paper templates the
size of each frame. Affix the selected
photocopies to them, so that you
can get a sense of how the images
will look once they're matted.

three Use the painter's tape and the templates to experiment with different arrangements on the wall. Try to keep the same distance between the frames.

four To place the picture hooks, measure and mark X's on the paper templates (see page 18). Hammer nails through the picture hooks (and the paper), then rip away the paper.

memory walls

COMMEMORATE A SPECIAL OCCASION BY PUTTING YOUR PHOTO ALBUM ON DISPLAY. FILL A WALL WITH IDENTICALLY FRAMED IMAGES, OR CREATE YOUR OWN SOUVENIR WALL, AND WATCH MEMORIES COME TO LIFE.

matching frames, varying mats

15 black, thin-edge frames, 11 x 18 in (28 x 45 cm) each • 15 white mats, with portrait, landscape, and mail-slot openings

• Matched frames are a clean way to display a large collection of photographs. Use this technique to show off wedding photos, commemorate baby's first year, or display photos of friends growing up together. To add interest to the pace of your display, vary the style of mats — portrait, landscape, or horizontal openings — but not the mat material.

• Choose a location and place three dramatic images in the center to establish a focal point. Add rows, placing frames three inches (7.5 cm) apart on all sides, to form a rectangle.

souvenir wall

24-in (60-cm) branching twig or piece of driftwood • 4 small binder clips or round paper clips • pushpins

• Tack a branching twig or a slim piece of driftwood to the wall and use it as a casual display rail for snapshots.
• Clip snapshots to the twig, or use pushpins for driftwood. Let photos hang above and below the twig for added drama.

desktop collage

ADD A LITTLE CREATIVE INSPIRATION TO YOUR WORKSPACE. DESIGN
A COLLAGE OF FAVORITE SNAPSHOTS, ADD A CLEAR COVER, AND TURN
YOUR DESKTOP INTO A PORTFOLIO OF EXPERIENCES AND IDEAS.

photos under plexiglas

• Pressure can adhere photos
to a surface, so allow some space
between the photos and the
plexiglas or acrylic sheet.
• To prevent cleaning solution
from making contact with the
photos, spray it onto a cloth,
never directly on the glass.

designing a snapshot collage

**plexiglas or acrylic sheet, cut to fit a desktop • small clear acrylic discs
to raise sheet above photos**

• Choose snapshots from your collection that inspire, amuse,
or conjure memories, and make the layout more intriguing by
enlarging some photos on a color copier. Tile pictures in rows
or a geometric pattern, or layer the images.

• Place acrylic discs at each desk corner and set the sheet of
plexiglas or acrylic on top. Or, suspend the sheet above the desk
using three evenly spaced rows of three-inch metal pipe fittings.

• You can also use a clear cutting board, tile, or even a
collector's magnifying glass to add a collage to part of the desk.

BEACH DAVID MORGAN

SPECIAL TECHNIQUES FOR displaying photos

USE CREATIVE PRESENTATION TO MAKE THE MOST OF EVERY PHOTO, AND TURN A WALL INTO AN ARTFUL STATEMENT

Different combinations of frames and mats, along with their placement, can redefine the way an image is perceived. For example, a small image set within a diminutive gold frame and tucked away on a shelf will have a far different impact than the same image displayed in a large frame with a wide mat and hung over the living room sofa.

A well-chosen frame distinguishes an image from the space around it, directing the eye to key elements of the photo. Frames come in various shapes and sizes, and each creates a subtly different effect. For vintage appeal, try placing a family portrait in an embellished frame with decorative carvings. Frames that extend out from an image on a level plane create a modern look. Dark mats focus attention on the picture, while reflective frames draw attention to the edges of the image. Wood frames highlight warm tones, while silver frames emphasize cool ones.

BRING PHOTOS OUT WHERE YOU'LL APPRECIATE THEM – AND WHERE THEY'LL HAVE THE MOST IMPACT

Photos can merge seamlessly with their surroundings or can offer a dramatic point of interest. The mat – the material (usually a piece of cardboard) between the picture and the frame – offers an easy tool to change the perception of an image. Use the size and cut of the mat to direct the eye: colored and layered mats add depth and intensify images. In a whole-wall display, mats with openings of different sizes create a sense of movement.

Depending on where they are placed, photos can set off the contour of furnishings and highlight or camouflage architectural features. As a rule of thumb, place the largest frames at the base of any display and smaller frames at the top. Enhance a ledge display by bringing some images forward and leaning others against the wall. You can do this by suspending a length of wire just below the ledge and attaching photos with clips, as shown at right, or by affixing photos directly to the lip of the ledge.

Photos are hung from the front of ledges (right) and layered to give this display added dimension and interest.

USE THE RIGHT TOOLS AND ORGANIZING SAVVY TO GET YOUR DESKTOP STUDIO UP AND RUNNING IN NO TIME

Setting up a home digital photo studio has never been easier. A digital camera, a computer, and photo software are the givens, along with a photo printer and a surge-protected power supply. Printers run the gamut from dedicated, photo-only models, which can print photo lab-quality snapshots, to photo-quality inkjet printers, which produce good-quality prints and can print larger formats as well as snapshot size.

You'll also want some storage space for ink cartridges, and file storage for photo-quality paper. Keep postcard and greeting card photo paper on hand to encourage creative projects. A high-capacity memory card is a good idea, as is an extra set of rechargeable camera batteries. If your photo library is very large, you can buy extra storage space online, or free up space on your hard drive by storing digital photos on discs.

Save digital images on discs (left), sorted by year, event, or holiday; then label each disc case with a thumbnail printout of its contents.

DECORATE YOUR WALLS BY GROUPING A SERIES OF PHOTOS TO CAPTURE SPECIAL MOMENTS OR EVENTS

Depending on how you hang them, groups of photos can relay a story in countless ways. For the best placement, hang photos at eye level and aim for a balance of small and large pieces. Horizontal groupings can make a narrow space seem wider. Use the room's architecture, such as trim and moldings, to guide your placement. Displays precisely aligned at the top or bottom have a symmetrical effect that calls attention to the progression of images. Stacking photos in a slightly asymmetrical grouping is another way to draw attention to a display, as is including a shadowbox or a three-dimensional object.

A few hints: try not to position photos in full sun, high-traffic areas, or humid conditions, or closer than eight inches (20 cm) from the tops of furnishings. If you can't avoid placing images near windows, use frames with UV-protective glass, which screens out ultraviolet rays. Also look for frame hangers, which are sturdier than traditional wall hangers, and felt disks, which protect walls and frames from scratches and nicks.

Symmetrical photo display (top); asymmetrical photo display (middle); photo display with shadowbox (bottom); horizontally aligned photo display (opposite)

USE TOGGLE HOOKS FROM A BOAT OR SEEK OUT
A POSTCARD RACK TO CREATE A UNIQUE SNAPSHOT
GALLERY THAT'S EASY TO UPDATE EVERY DAY

BARRAGAN

Provence Interiors

TRICIA GUILD'S COUNTRY COLOR

snapshot solution

SNAPSHOTS HAVE WONDERFUL STORIES TO TELL. YET WHEN THEY'RE FRAMED ALONE, THEY CAN BE TOO SMALL TO CAPTURE ATTENTION. HERE'S HOW TO GIVE THEM THE COLORFUL PRESENCE THEY DESERVE.

displaying photos by color

2 poster frames, 22 x 28 in (56 x 71 cm) • poster board or gator board (sold in art-supply stores) • archival glue • brayer • measuring tape

Arranging pictures by color not only gives them visual unity (which can be hard to achieve with snapshots), it also breaks the narrative out of the ho-hum, "and-here's-another-view-of-the-scenery" tradition. If your snapshot collection is running wild despite your best efforts, here's a fun solution that you can complete in just one afternoon.

Cover a table with newspaper and unearth all the color snapshots that never made it into frames or albums. Sort the images by dominant color, whether the blue of water and sky, or the bright splash of color from that red shirt you wore everywhere last year.

photo adhesives

● Photo-safe adhesives include archival-quality photo corners, acid-free linen and paper tape, archival glue, and wheat- and rice-starch pasted hinges (which are the best option for fragile, valuable images).

● Do not use cellophane tape, rubber cement, or any hobby glue to adhere photos to a backing. All will eventually damage photos.

one Sort pictures by their
dominant color, making separate
stacks for each hue. The more you
can mix people, places, and things
within each stack, the better.

two Try a rough layout on poster
board or gator board (depending
on the depth of the frame). Use
layering to "crop" photos and
highlight the most interesting details.

three When you like the arrangement, use archival glue or photo tape to affix the images to the poster or gator board. Roll the edges gently with a brayer to adhere.

four Let dry overnight, then set the finished collage in the poster frame and measure from the frame to the wire as shown, for placement on the wall (see page 18 for tips).

SMALL OR LARGE, THE BEST FRAMES GRACEFULLY
ATTRACT ATTENTION, SUBTLY MAKE A PHOTO MORE
STRIKING, AND PLACE FOCUS ON THE IMAGE

lighting photo displays

GIVE YOUR FAVORITE PHOTOGRAPHS THE SPOTLIGHT THEY DESERVE.
WELL-PLANNED PICTURE LIGHTING LETS ARTWORK SHINE IN THE
EVENING AND HELPS YOU GET THE MOST FROM A DISPLAY.

gallery lighting for photos

2 wood frames, 16 x 20 in (40 x 50 cm) • 2 adjustable gallery lights

- Like people, pictures tend to look best when the light around them is flattering. The goal is to provide even illumination across the entire image while protecting it from heat. Cool and color-correct, low-wattage halogen is perfect for lighting art.

- Position gallery lights far enough above each photo so that the arc of light covers the entire image. You may need multiple fixtures to evenly illuminate a large display.

- Keep the focus on the photos rather than the lights by selecting fixtures with a finish that is neutral or that matches the wall.

- Use a bulb that is brighter than the overall light in the room to help the image stand out.

photo lighting ideas

- Set at a safe distance, votives or tealights enhance the play of light and shadow in black-and-white photos.
- Spotlights and track lights offer precise lighting from a distance; battery-powered frame-mount lights make it easy to change the location of art without changing the lighting.

modern nostalgia

-FRAMES AND MATS CAN WORK WONDERS TO UNIFY A COLLECTION OF OLD AND NEW IMAGES. USE MATCHING FRAMES TO HELP VINTAGE PICTURES BLEND WITH CONTEMPORARY PHOTOS AND SURROUNDINGS.

restoring old photos

• With the widespread availability of digital technology, scanning and reprinting photos has never been easier.

• Most copy and photo centers will work with you to eliminate spots, tears, and color deterioration. If you have a computer and a scanner/printer, you can do it yourself.

mixing vintage and new photos

color-coordinated frames in assorted sizes and mat widths • wall ledges

• Treasured photos are often an eclectic mix of sizes, styles, and vintages. If your mix of portraits ranges from tintypes to toddler pictures, span the decades by setting them in modern frames. The key lies in keeping frame color and finish within a limited palette — like the dark wood, black, and silver frames shown here — but varying frame size and mat width for interest.

• Lean the collection on wall ledges for a modern effect. Let pictures overlap, and break boundaries from one ledge to the next. Set a row of pictures on the floor to complete the display.

collector's gallery

COLLECTIONS MAKE INTERIORS MORE INTRIGUING. IF PICTURES ARE
YOUR PASSION, TRANSFORM A ROOM INTO YOUR OWN PERSONAL
GALLERY WITH THESE SIMPLE DISPLAY TRICKS.

spacing and display techniques

**assortment of framed images: family photos • portraits • landscape
photos • enlargements • snapshots • posters**

- Each person's collection is different, but a few simple rules
of thumb apply to all gallery displays:

- Pairs and groups of three are the most visually pleasing.

- Don't hang pictures too high. Place the central images at eye
level, or a little higher if the ceiling is lofty, to create a focal point.
Center a trio of images on the wall, one to two inches (2.5–5 cm)
apart, and work outward to form a rough square or rectangle.

- Balance heavy with light. Group small frames together to offset
the visual weight of a single large image.

collector's boxes

- Vitrines and curio boxes are
clever ways to display heirloom
photos, whether locket photos
or other vintage portraits.
- Emphasize a theme by
displaying objects with photos.
Antique cameras, pocket watches,
and pictures all offer a nostalgic
look back in time.

CHILDREN GROWING UP, A SPECIAL EVENT,
A CHRONICLE OF FRIENDS AND FAMILY — PHOTOS
CONNECT US WITH PAST, PRESENT, AND FUTURE

shelf motif

TO MIX PHOTOS AND OBJECTS IN A COHESIVE DISPLAY, START WITH THE
SECRET THAT EVERY ART STUDENT LEARNS: STICK TO WHITE-ON-WHITE
FOR A QUIET APPEAL THAT HIGHLIGHTS PATTERN, LINE, AND SHAPE.

unifying a collection with white

3 black-and-white photos • 2 white frames, 8 x 10 in (20 x 25 cm) •
1 white frame, 24 x 24 in (60 x 60 cm) • white mats • white shelves
and objects

• When you combine pictures and curios, you're also combining
shapes. Keep the whole display a single color to highlight
similarities and unify the composition.

• Create a sense of rhythm from shelf to shelf by alternating
tall pieces with shorter ones.

• Surround black-and-white photos with an all-white collection
to create an interesting textural background for the images.

• Shelves allow photos to be set higher and lower than they
might ordinarily be hung, adding an element of surprise.

photos and light

• In monochromatic displays,
such as this one, choose graphic,
high-contrast photos that are easy
to discern from a distance.
• Try not to position furnishings
so that a shelf display is wider
than a piece of furniture directly
below it. If your display is
narrower, it should be at least
half the width of a piece below it.

mirror images

SIMPLE TO ASSEMBLE AND EASY TO CHANGE ON A WHIM, PHOTO COLLAGES PRESENTED ON A MIRROR OR WITHIN AN EMPTY FRAME HAVE A RELAXED APPEAL AND INVITE YOU TO UPDATE THE DISPLAY OVER TIME.

uncovered photos

• Dust unframed pictures with a lint-free silk cloth. Do not rub, as this will drive dirt particles further into the paper and possibly scratch the surface.

• Use photo corners to affix photos directly to the mirror glass, which keeps the photo edges from curling.

using mirrors as frames

mirror with wide, white wood frame, 14 x 18 in (36 x 45 cm) • linen or paper photo tape • scrapbook stickers

• Mirrors are a natural base for a photo collage. Use a single large mirror to display a mix of photos, or collect several hand mirrors and use them to display vintage family photos.

• Attach images with photo tape, or fasten photo corners directly to the glass. You can also use stick-on letters, tiny frames, and other embellishments designed for albums and scrapbook pages.

• Preserve vintage photographs by displaying photocopies, which you can layer and embellish without worry. Archive the originals in acid-neutral photo albums or storage boxes.

MAKE A DESK OR TABLETOP INSPIRING WITH
A LAMINATED COLLAGE OF VACATION POSTCARDS
OR A LAYERED DISPLAY OF FAMILY PHOTOS

seasonal shadowbox

PART PICTURE FRAME, PART CURIO CABINET, A TABLETOP SHADOWBOX
IS AN IDEAL PLACE FOR ALL THE LITTLE KEEPSAKES, PICTURES, AND
COLLECTIONS THAT CELEBRATE EACH PASSING SEASON.

holiday photos

- Keep holiday trimmings from becoming the focus of photos by shooting outside, against a clean, graphic background, such as a snowy landscape.
- If you are taking a photo with decorations as a backdrop, zoom in enough to eliminate distracting ornaments from the periphery.

displaying photos with keepsakes

assorted holiday photographs, cards, and ornaments • tabletop shadowbox • small round mirror

- From holiday cards to vacation snapshots, each season has its treasures we can't resist collecting. Instead of stacking mementos on your desk or bureau, set them in a shadowbox for all to enjoy.

- For a dynamic display, place larger items at the center to create a focal point, and then add smaller pieces – in pairs or groups of three – to fill the frame.

- Layer flat and three-dimensional objects, but leave some space between items here and there.

- Photos are sensitive to heat and light, so make copies and store originals if the shadowbox is near a fireplace or in full sun.

September 2004

March 2005

July 2003

May 2002

August 2001

photo growth chart

CHILDREN SEEM TO GROW BY LEAPS AND BOUNDS OVERNIGHT.
CAPTURE ALL THEIR AGES AND STAGES WITH A PHOTO GROWTH
CHART THAT, IF ONLY FOR A MOMENT, STOPS TIME IN ITS TRACKS.

narrative display

frames, 5 x 7 in (13 x 18 cm) • carpenter's ruler • picture hangers

• Start by fastening a carpenter's ruler securely to the wall, or paint a measuring stick motif on the wall. Measure your child at four- to six-month intervals throughout the year, marking the height on the ruler with white tape or a permanent marker.

• Next to the mark, attach a framed snapshot taken at the same time. Label the frame with the date, month, or season, alternating horizontal and vertical portraits to give the finished display a sense of movement.

• Narrative displays tell a story: substitute a timeline for the ruler and adapt this project to show the progression of a special event, such as a wedding, anniversary, or graduation day.

portrait-taking tips

• To get a great portrait, professional photographers advise coming in close enough to fill the whole frame with your child's image.

• Here's another tip from the experts: keep the subject slightly off-center in the frame to create a more interesting portrait.

PLEASURE OF decorating with photos

DRAW FROM YOUR MEMORIES, PASSIONS,
AND HOBBIES TO CHOOSE PHOTOS THAT
ACCENT, OR TRANSFORM, EVERY ROOM

Photo displays offer a vast scrapbook of experiences, but they also add color, drama, and scale to a room. If you taped life-size posters all over your bedroom walls as a child, you've experienced the way a photo arrangement can transform a room. A well-placed image can provide a small room with a vista, make narrow spaces seem wider, and make low-ceilinged spaces seem taller.

More often than not, a room's furnishings — sofas, sconces, and media equipment — have already claimed a good portion of wall space. But that's no reason to live with blank walls. Tuck a row of small pictures under a window, lean a tall frame at the end of a hall, or create a gallery stepping up a stairwell. Whether the images are calm or active, large or small, the only trick is finding creative new ways to display them.

COMPOSE A GALLERY-STYLE ARRANGEMENT THAT'S AN EVER-CHANGING WORK OF ART

The beauty of a photo gallery is that it lets you change a display over time. A simple way around putting holes in the wall is to range pictures along a ledge or countertop, or to simply lean them on a wall. A row of matched frames creates an orderly presentation that's pleasing to the eye, especially in a hallway. However you choose to group them, most displays are variations on one of these classic shapes: block, in which the outer perimeter forms a square, rectangle, or diamond shape; mosaic, in which pictures large and small cluster around three images at center; and gallery, in which frames are set in a row and aligned at the top, bottom, or center.

Here's a quick primer on hooks. Traditional hook picture hangers work best with drywall and plaster. Professional picture hangers have thin, sharp nails that penetrate walls easily. Use sawtooth hangers for small, light pictures, and frame hangers at the top corners of heavy pieces. Wall-cleat (or French-cleat) systems work well for heavier artwork.

Decorate with photos by creating a hallway gallery (opposite); tucking snapshots in unexpected places (top); or using colorful tacks to frame an informal collage (bottom).

SHARE THE MEMORIES: DISPLAY SNAPSHOTS
WITH MEMENTOS, OR MAKE A TIDY FAN DECK
BY CLIPPING THEM TOGETHER WITH A RING

ribbon displays

BEFORE THE LATE NINETEENTH CENTURY, PICTURES WERE OFTEN DISPLAYED ON A STRIP OF RIBBON HUNG FROM A PICTURE RAIL. THIS PROJECT TAKES A MODERN APPROACH TO ACHIEVE THE SAME EFFECT.

creating a changeable display

4 framed pictures • 1 small empty frame • 1 large empty frame • 5 ft (1.5 m) shaker tape or canvas webbing • upholstery tacks • drapery hooks • measuring tape • hammer • picture nails

This project relies on Shaker tape, a heavy-duty canvas strip traditionally used to weave chair seats. Craft, sewing, and upholstery supply stores usually stock the tape. Unless your pictures are very light, resist the temptation to use ribbon. Shaker tape is stronger, and you can pierce it without causing it to tear or fray. Best of all, you can change the display easily, without making new holes in the wall: just lift off the pictures and move the drapery hooks. Hang a single strip as shown, flank a doorway with a matched pair, or place several side by side to fill up a wall.

choosing frames

- Frames change the way pictures look: dark frames make them appear more vibrant, and reflective frames draw attention to the edges of the image.
- Create an interesting effect by surrounding a small framed photo with a larger empty frame instead of a mat.

one Calculate the length of the
display by arranging pictures as
shown and measuring. Add 1 foot
(30 cm), cut the tape to that length,
and finish the bottom with a V-cut.

two To create a decorative
hanger, loop the tape through the
small empty frame, curling the cut
end beneath the loop. Affix the tape
to the frame with drapery tacks.

three Lay the tape and pictures on a table and use a tape measure to help evenly space the frames. Attach drapery hooks to the tape at regular intervals.

four Hang the tape on the wall and then position the frames on the drapery hooks. If a picture leans forward, staple its frame to the tape from the back.

custom fit

PROTECT ORIGINALS AND FIT YOUR PHOTOS INTO READY-MADE FRAMES
WITH THIS STYLIST'S TRICK: USE A COPY MACHINE TO ENLARGE OR
SHRINK THE IMAGE, THEN TRIM THE RESULT TO THE PERFECT SIZE.

copying photos

photo frame mirror or wood photo frame, 3 x 4 in (7.5 x 10 cm) •
12-in (30-cm) length of twill tape • wooden tassel

• Start with a professional-quality copier and clean glass. Some copy centers and photo stores offer archival-quality copiers, which print at higher resolution to make better copies.

• To improve the clarity and resolution of a copy, try using a copier to reduce a photo by ten percent. Copy your photos onto heavy white cardstock, or try neutral tints to create artistic effects.

• Trim the photocopy to fit the frame. Add an element of surprise to coat hooks or a mirror in an entry hall by using them to display a photo. Add a length of twill tape and a wooden tassel to embellish a small framed picture, as shown opposite.

household photos

• Use family photos to bring organization to an entry hall, kitchen office, or other busy hub of your home. Place each family member's photo next to that person's own key hook or mail slot. Or, use a photo of the house to label house keys, car photos to identify car keys, and so on.

sequence secrets

IF YOU HAVE A SERIES OF IMAGES YOU LOVE, GIVE THEM A DRAMATIC STAGE. PLACE COLORFUL FRAMES AGAINST A DARK BACKGROUND TO CREATE A SOPHISTICATED DISPLAY WITH ART-STUDIO STYLE.

photo mats

- Always use an acid-neutral mat when framing a valuable picture. Matting around a framed photo creates a pocket of air between the photo and the glass. With matting, the framed picture won't wrinkle or stick to the glass as a result of temperature and humidity changes.

designing a photo sequence

6 black-and-white photos depicting a sequence • 6 thin-edge red frames, 16 x 18 in (40 x 45 cm) • 6 beige, acid-neutral mats

- To make a sequence of photos into a polished art installation, take cues from museum galleries, which rely on high-contrast backgrounds and precise alignment to make artworks arresting. Matched frames and mats in aligned rows draw attention to the natural movement within the photos.

- Lay out the sequence so that the photos create a rhythm — alternate dark and light, or mix close-ups with long-range images. Sometimes a sequential order works the best, and sometimes an out-of-order placement makes everything more interesting.

MATCH THE SHAPES OF PHOTOS TO THE SPACE,
AND DISPLAY THEM WHERE THEY ARE LEAST
EXPECTED — UNDER A WINDOW OR ABOVE A SINK

PICTURES CLIPPED TO A LENGTH OF LINE
IN AN EASY-TO-CHANGE DISPLAY TAKE CUES
FROM A PHOTOGRAPHER'S DARKROOM

ladder layout

LEDGES AND LADDERS ARE AN INVITATION TO TAKE A CLOSER LOOK
AT WHAT'S ON DISPLAY. THEY'RE ALSO AN OPPORTUNITY TO MINGLE
PICTURES AND COLLECTIONS — OFTEN WITH INTRIGUING RESULTS.

cropping photos

• If black-and-white photos look
a bit old-fashioned, new crops
can frequently make them seem
livelier and more dynamic.
• Try cropping out the "empty"
space at the top and bottom of
portraits, and on either side
of landscape photos.

layering a photo display

black-and-white photos in assorted subjects and sizes • silver, black,
and wood thin-edge frames in assorted sizes • wall ledges or ladders

• Instead of hanging pictures here and there, and having books,
magazines, and collectibles scattered about the room, corral these
items in a ladder display whose sum becomes greater than its
parts. Ladder displays are engaging because they're accessible;
the objects they hold can be picked up and examined. They also
make it easy to change a display without putting holes in the wall.

• Start by placing taller, larger pictures in the back and cluster
smaller pieces around them. Let photographs and mementos play
off each other in interesting ways. For example, place a poster
from a trip with a souvenir and photos from the same vacation.

poster presentation

ENLARGED PHOTOS OR ART PRINTS CAN BE STRIKING ADDITIONS TO A ROOM'S DECOR. USE THEM FRAMED OR UNFRAMED AS A FOCAL POINT OR AS A CLEVER ALTERNATIVE TO A HEADBOARD.

sketchbook arrangement

1 wide-edge black frame .
2 medium-edge dark wood frames .
5 thin-edge frames in assorted finishes and sizes

• Line up your images art-school style, so the frames are touching and the effect is that of an open sketchbook. Create a central axis by aligning photos along a center line, rather than making the edges of the frames line up.

creating art prints

3 high-quality art prints or enlarged photos • T-pins

• Poster-size images, whether art prints or enlargements of your own photos, are a near-instant decorating technique that transforms a blank wall into a bold statement.

• The prints shown at right, called kallitypes or Van Dyke prints, rely on a process involving light-sensitive salts. The popularly available "sun print" kits create the same look but in smaller sizes.

• For a similar effect, consider having a sepia enlargement made at a local copy center. Digital technology makes it possible to have almost any image in your collection retouched, colorized, or made sepia, then printed in an enlarged version.

photos in kids' rooms

KIDS BOUNCE AROUND, AND OFTEN THEIR BELONGINGS DO, TOO.
A MAGNETIC PHOTO STRIP CAN KEEP A GROWING GALLERY OF
ACHIEVEMENTS AND SCHOOL PICTURES SAFELY ABOVE THE FRAY.

scrapbook strip for kids

magnetic strip • paper frames, tags, and labels • photo magnets

- Providing children with a place to show off their photos, drawings, and accomplishments is more than a fun way to decorate – it also builds self-esteem and encourages creativity.

- Hang a long magnetic or corkboard strip at child height to make a flexible system for an evolving display. Use paper-clip magnets to hold pictures and mementos securely.

- Mirror the casual style of this arrangement by placing images both above and below the strip's border.

- Surround photos with a bright color, especially one that's in the image. To do this, you can use a colored mat or a painted wall.

candid photos

- The secret to taking good candid shots is to capture your subject in action.
- A few more tips: avoid having large shapes or colorful objects in the picture's edge; shoot in good light, but away from lamps or direct sunlight; and brace your elbows on your body to steady the camera.

hallway gallery

A HALLWAY SHOULD BE MORE THAN SIMPLY A PLACE TO PASS THROUGH. HUNG IN AN ORDERED COLLECTION ALONG A WALL, RELATED IMAGES AND HEIRLOOMS TELL A CAPTIVATING STORY.

photos and mementos

● In a themed display, you can alternate pictures with related objects to strengthen the overall presentation. For example, hang your grandmother's mirror next to one of her framed letters, or place your father's camera case on a ledge underneath his photograph.

designing a hallway display

3 narrow-edge black frames in different sizes • 2 wide-edge black frames in different sizes • 2 mirrors in different sizes

● Choose a frame as a primary focal point, and group the others around it. You can visually link any display by hanging the images close together, so the pieces read as a whole.

● Alternate pictures with objects. Reinforce the idea that the items belong together by choosing a group of frames and objects that have similarities in color, texture, or material.

● Frames need not all match exactly. In fact, having different sizes and weights will lend a feeling of energy to the presentation.

staircase studio

A STAIRWAY IS THE PERFECT PLACE TO HANG A DISPLAY OF FAVORITE PORTRAITS OR FRAMED PHOTOS OF CHILDREN, TRACING THE PASSAGE OF TIME FROM PRESCHOOL TODDLER TO COLLEGE GRADUATE.

hanging a stepped display

assorted portraits • dark wooden frames in various finishes and sizes

● Stairways are ready-made display spaces, equipped with two key things a successful photo gallery requires: plenty of open wall space and lots of foot traffic. Make yours a place to linger and admire by decorating it with a stepped photo display.

● Align the center points of the pictures diagonally, following the line of the stairs and the upward pitch of the staircase.

● The steeper the angle upward, the more pictures can be stepped top and bottom.

● Use a stairway display to trace the passage of time, with pictures of a child growing up or holidays through the years.

finding space

2 black, medium-edge frames, 6 x 6 in (15 x 15 cm) • 2 blue linen mats • monofilament thread

● Pictures and picture hangers usually go together, but this inventive technique keeps walls free of holes and uses stairwell space to advantage.

● Attach twin frames together with monofilament thread draped over a flat railing, then enjoy the view from either side.

stealing the scene

COLOR ENERGIZES PHOTOS, WHETHER ON THE WALL OR IN A FRAMED
MAT. YOU CAN USE COLOR TO MAKE A SUBTLE PICTURE MORE DRAMATIC
OR HELP A DRAMATIC IMAGE STEAL THE SCENE.

picture height

- Placing photos low on a wall or in shelves will make ceilings appear higher, drawing attention to the images rather than the room. The faux "window" of a color photograph, placed at the end of a room, can also make a space appear larger.

combining pictures and color

4 narrow-edge black frames, 9 x 12 in (23 x 30 cm) • 4 white mats

- Background wall color plays a key role in the way photographs look. Take a hint from museums and galleries and use wall color to highlight accent colors that might otherwise fade away in a photo and to make a photo display more subtle or dramatic.

- Keep in mind that the narrower the frame and mat, the more the wall color will influence the appearance of the picture.

- Frame colors matter, too. Gold emphasizes warm hues in both picture and wall, while silver brings out cool tones. Black and dark wood accent the color in a photograph.

A WHOLE NEW WORLD OF ideas for photos

USE EVERYDAY OBJECTS IN NEW WAYS TO CHANGE THE WHOLE NOTION OF WHAT A PHOTO FRAME SHOULD BE

Now that you've mastered frames and mats of all shapes and sizes, have a little fun with substitutes of your own invention. Anything that surrounds or suspends a photo can take the place of a frame, and opportunities for creative repurposing abound.

Borrow an empty glass storage jar or vase from the pantry, and use it to display a still life of photos and objects – a vacation snapshot amid shells you collected on the beach, for example. Back an ornate vintage frame with a sheet of clear acrylic or corkboard and use it as a casual photo bulletin board near a desk. Make clipboards into instant frames that allow you to change images whenever you choose. Or, hang up a photo series with clothespins or clip hangers. All make witty frame substitutes that surprise and intrigue.

CLEVER NEW WAYS TO USE PHOTOS, FROM DISPLAYS UNDER GLASS TO PLACE CARDS AND LABELS

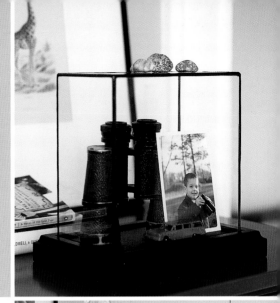

Photo displays are as much a source of fun and amusement as they are a balance of shape and scale. Aim for the element of surprise by converting everyday objects into photo frames and hangers. Simply stroll around the house and give your imagination free rein – you'll be surprised by what you dream up.

Try using place-card holders instead of frames for snapshots. Or, hang up a magnetic strip and use it to display a changing array of photos. Anything that can grip the edge of a photo can become its frame or hanger, from colorful metal binder clips to the tiny bamboo pins traditionally used to hold drying pen-and-ink drawings. Tell a story by mixing photos and objects, highlight your treasures with wit, and use your photos to create rooms full of discovery.

Use place-card holders to display photos, or let photos themselves serve as place cards (opposite). Display a childhood photo of a loved one with cherished toys in a vitrine or collector's box (top). Protect a copied photo from the humidity of the bath in a covered vase (middle). Use photos as labels, or simply to hide the contents, in jars of dry goods (bottom).

TO MAKE A UNIQUE PRESENTATION OF YOUR
TREASURED SNAPSHOTS, USE A MUSIC STAND,
LADDER, OR OTHER FOUND OBJECT AS A FRAME

creating a photo grid

TURN SOUVENIR SNAPSHOTS OR PICTURE POSTCARDS INTO
A WORK OF ART. MOUNT YOUR IMAGES IN A GRAPHIC GRID
THAT CELEBRATES WARM CLIMATES AND SUNNY SKIES.

preparing the photos

20 color snapshots or picture postcards • sheet of gator board (sold at art-supply stores) • cutting mat • cutting knife • archival spray glue • tissue paper • brayer • package of adhesive velcro strips

Before you begin, have a set of double prints made from your original photos, in case you make a mistake. Consider converting your images to digital format, especially if you are working with postcards, so you can easily change their size. If you already have digital photos, print them out as four-inch (10-cm) squares.

This grid technique lends itself to many different hanging configurations: depending on available wall space, you can use more photos to build a larger grid; create a longer, narrower shape; or set photos in a neat row at chair-rail height.

unframed photos

• The context of the grid automatically lends presence to unframed photos, so no additional framing is needed.
• You can stick to snapshots from a single trip, mix favorite images together, or assign each row a theme, such as streets, houses, and doorways, or land, sea, and sky.

one Print digital pictures as
four-inch (10-cm) squares (shown)
or trim 4 x 6 in (10 x15 cm) prints
into squares. Cover a table with
newspaper and lay out your photos.

two Use spray archival glue to
adhere the photos to the gator
board. (You can change the order
later.) Cover the photos with tissue
paper and roll with the brayer.

three Use the measurements on the cutting mat as a guide to help you trim mounted photos. For clean edges, keep the blade at a 90-degree angle to the board.

four Affix the soft-loop sides of the Velcro strips to the backs of the photos. Affix the stiff-hook sides to the wall, five inches (13 cm) apart, forming a grid. Attach the images.

photo labels

LET PICTURES SPEAK A THOUSAND WORDS BY USING THEM IN PLACE OF WRITTEN LABELS. IDENTIFY PHOTO ALBUMS WITH A PEEK AT WHAT'S INSIDE, AND USE SNAPSHOT TAGS FOR EVERYTHING.

carbon copies

snapshots of office supplies • color copier • colored paper

• Bring a touch of wit to your work area (and never hunt for supplies again) by using photocopied snapshots to label stored objects.

• Snap Polaroids or digital images of office supplies from paper clips to scissors, then use a copier to enlarge and transfer images to colored paper.

organizing with photos

photocopy enlargements of snapshots, 8½ x 11 in (22 x 28 cm) • photo albums or ring binders

• Cut copies of photographs into strips lengthwise, and use them to identify the contents of a photo album or ring binder.

• Copy the photo strips onto card stock to give them body, then glue them to the photo albums' spine, or insert them in the binders' spine pocket.

• This system of labeling not only keeps shelves organized, it also neatly combines storage and display.

• Make a photo montage with different images, or enlarge a single photo, cut it into strips, and mount each to the spine of a different album or binder for a split-image triptych.

MIX ITEMS AT HAND IN UNEXPECTED WAYS: SHOWCASE PHOTOS ON LEDGES OR SNAPSHOTS IN ORNATE FRAMES

INDEX